ANGELS AT BUS STOPS

ANGELS AT BUS STOPS

poems

Jon Veinberg

LYNX HOUSE PRESS
Spokane, Washington

ACKNOWLEDGEMENTS

Askew: " Chess," " Flies," "Dog with Dementia"

Chicago Quarterly Review: "The Ethereal Coffeemaker," "Stealing Pomegranates"

Corners of the Mouth: A Celebration of Thirty Years at the Annual San Luis Obispo Poetry Festival: "Pigeon in a Palm Tree at Roeding Park"

HUBBUB: "The Owl Express," "Pumpernickel," "Woman at a Red Table"

Miramar: "3 Trees," "Angels at Bus Stops," "The Birth of Light," "Forest in Twilight," "Jesus at the Ride and Shine," "Saint John of the Salamanders," "A Small Suitcase," "Topiary," "Wild Birds," "Wind"

New Letters: "The Bill Collector at Sunrise"

One For The Money: The Sentence as a Poetic Form: "The Mad Woman's Harp"

The Packinghouse Review: "Blackberries," "Fleeing Estonia"

Redactions: Poetry, Poetics, & Prose: "The German Shepherd Blues"

San Pedro Review: "House with Unmowed Lawn"

Stringtown: "You Walk with the Spirits."

Tar River Poetry: "When Salvador Dali Camped on My Roof"

Heartfelt thanks to Christopher Buckley and Dixie Salazar for their dogged support and insightful suggestions.

Cover Art: Re-Entry by Mel McCudden. Other paintings by Mel McCudden may be found online at artspiritgallery.com

Author Photo: Dixie Salazar.

Book Design: Christine Holbert.

FIRST EDITION

Cataloging-in-Publication Data is available from the Library of Congress.

ISBN 978-0-8992413-7-1

CONTENTS

I

II

III

IV

This book is for Christopher Buckley, true poet and friend, and for Katrin, õde

JESUS AT THE RIDE AND SHINE

August and the air so still
you can hear flies stubbling
the windshields
and the snap of towels
cracking a target of ants
jacketing a floorboard
of gum wrappers
and Watchtower pamphlets.
Then the deep pause
that measures the sun
blessing the rough as rye
tar of Blackstone Avenue,
floating from the eyes of Johnny,
Nacho, Etroy, the sly dreamer,
or whoever chips in for canned mackerel
on discounted bread for lunch,
and an occasional game
of fifty cent nine-ball
on Saturday after work.
We knew it was him
by the ruffled and blemished robe,
nothing a little Miracle cleanser
couldn't fix,
that stray strap of sandal
bitten off at its sole,
the wind swept chaos of hair,
and by the 3D post cards handed out
to us by Gramma Solis
on her Sunday visits to the Hall,

and the photo of him
thumb tacked to the wall
of everyone's kitchen nook of long ago
where he is the target of light
flanked by mostly old shits
at a long bulky table,
whose firebrand hands are hiding,
or complaining about the lack of meat
for dinner, his eyes, then as now,
as calm as Millerton Lake at twilight
as if they were folded
into something lost beyond
the horizon's ridge,
a ship, perhaps, veiled by sagging
clouds that outweigh the sky,
and as confused by the green-
finned Falcon and debit cards only box
as we are of analog clocks. So
we play paper, rock, and scissors, to see
who among us will ride
through the tunnel with Jesus,
through antennae snap and hisses
from below the stones
of the conveyor belt and rollover
blast, and the chemical wash
of nozzles probing the tires,
and the hot white foam of soap
storming the windows until his eyes
turn as gray as a nightmare
of rotating scrubs and brushes
and I ask him to keep driving
through the parking lot,

toward the southbound freeway
until the dust chalk
no longer claims our faces
and I snip off the electronic monitor
as we loll through the valley,
white stars of cotton at our backs
and I teach Jesus how not to brake
on the curves until we hear the sea
ringing in our ears, children
playing tag with the tide, bums
roasting onions on make-shift grills
and the gulls ripping open
another bag of Doritos. I could go
on like this forever: Wind salt
and seaweed drafting my nostrils,
bossing Jesus to hold the wheel
a little tighter, a bowl of weed
in the glove compartment of a shiny
and towel-dried car, the mirror
steamed with excitement and a hope
grander than a gold, stolen Cadillac,
and in the distance the air full
of the shrill voiced solitude of seals.
And with the valley heat at my back
and Jesus' lantern blue eyes
taking in the blue sea,
my eternity's new playground roars.

WHEN SALVADOR DALI CAMPED ON MY ROOF

It was a good year for figs
and a summer of honey-melting heat
when my neighbors saw him
shackling himself to my chimney,
braiding twine to rope the clouds—
a band of jays shit on his cape
and not by accident stray cats
serenaded him from the bushes.
Let's get it right: T.V. antennas
were spider webs designed
originally as modern crucifixes.
Skateboards were wheelchairs
pumped up on amphetamines,
cars were elephants craving water,
all palm tress were phalluses
and from where he sat then
the stars were butterflies that
crisscrossed the sky and collided
for his pleasure only,
and through the night light
of my neighbor's house
a mattress sagged under
the weight of excessive loneliness.
We dusted off our lawn chairs,
hugged our children, short-leashed
our dogs to watch him raving
at the moon until my roof became
heaven's nightclub. We hosed
the roof to cool him down

and watched the heat rise from
shingle to shingle into cushions of mist.
We tried to talk him down.
We named our community garden
after him and had him sample the tomatoes.
We tossed him an alarm clock
so he could predict earthquakes
and laddered up to him a Bible a day
so he could continue to declare war
on death. One morning we found
him dead among the hydrangeas,
flattening the crabgrass, a shadow
of flies already feasting. We closed his
eyes but the lids kept popping open,
his face, a hodgepodge of crumpled maps.

SAINT JOHN OF THE SALAMANDERS

It was a fate worse
than getting slapped by Jesus,
watching those
maimed and severed bodies
colliding with each other
in slow motion,
under the glow of the wall clock,
above the ether scented lab desk
that shouldered
the unwashed sherry glasses.
Autumn's off-balanced
and slender agates,
born in camouflage to manzanita
and scrub oak,
partner to the chaparral stem
and at one with the green
scaled wetlands
that must have tasted
like the sweat of a young boy
running away from home
for the first time,
now spiraling into nothingness,
tumbling through
the rusted afternoon
into a stream of numbers
and Petri dishes,
into the hidden thrushes
of search and probability,
into an oblivion
greater than a horizon.
If it weren't for the eyes,

ink dappled and brass lidded,
eyes I bathed in saline
and can now sail a boat through,
or the fear I held
for all the lives you couldn't save
I would have boxed you up
when no one was looking,
dropped you off at the canal bank
among the casks
of abandoned cats
and dirt filmed whiskey bottles
to fend for yourself,
to dart through a nest of stones
for crickets and bloodworms,
dragging your hind leg
through the fire wheel of day
and gray weather,
shedding your tail at night
to the shadow of the owl's claw
traipsing the moon.
Log dweller, flame swallower,
elusive pet incapable
of plotting harm,
you weren't cut out for immortality
any more than the ragamuffin
child with nightmares
whose window pane you sprawl out on,
a froth of rain for your coat,
a cluster of clouds
and an implacable sky for your roof,
waiting for the earth
to open up a tiny crack
to bequeath your slough,
cinders of your existence.

JEFF FROM HEAVEN

I'll show you the ropes
when you get here
just like I did when you
walked into Miss Gardner's
fourth grade classroom,
shaggy-haired and lost
among a jungle of eyes
scoping you out. It
was so quiet I could hear
dust sighing on the windowsill . . .
From where I sit now,
with the sun's help, I can see
chocolate-colored bonanzas of
mushrooms big as pizza
platters sprouting on all the willows
and oaks and no one
gets poison ivy or goes hungry.
The air's so crisp
you could crack the sky
into a thousand heavens
by fanning the wind.
No helicopters here to rove
the clouds, coming back
with mangled Jesus bolts
and an unpiloted rotor.
No brownouts deviling
the night, stinging my eyes
into oblivion. No need
to poach cantaloupes under

a full moon or push my walker
down Fulton Street bumming
cigarettes from the runaways
loitering under the Sanctuary clock
tower. In the seam between
night and day, birds
come to sit on my shoulder,
birds as bright as
the kaleidoscope of rings
we window-shopped
down at the pawnshop,
so luminous it almost blinded us
into thievery. No more burnt
feet racing for squares of shade
across Tulare Street's summer
asphalt. No more tossed whiskey
bottles floating atop the duck blind.
No need to hunt, play poker or
learn magic because nothing disappears
up here. No catcalls or doorbells
to ring. I'll know when you're coming.
It'll be easier than your first
day of fourth grade.

WILD BIRDS

Beneath the tangle of drizzle and mist,
the wind hisses prophesies to itself,
muffling the pants of nose-to-the ground dogs
who just the hour before slipped their collars.

Why do I keep seeing you there, Omar,
on the corner of Broadway and Belmont
heeling your smokes and losing count of angels,
thumbing a ride under the funeral parlor's wink?

And the wild birds whose names are no longer within reach
that preened their wings inside your heart so nimbly
it is no small wonder to catch you floating among them
leaf-like, past the palm fronds and recalcitrant roses,

through the moon's braid of light beyond
where fog and poverty drip into the same alley
and when the blue tinderbox of desire crackles
outside the hospital you died in and the untamed soul teeters

like an unbalanced brick, I'm sure you'll turn up
through the gauze of clouds, the reef of time, to answer it all back
with spit and guts, the wind scorching your eyelid,
your hat on fire, your words melded in the hard flame of stars.

SAD ANGELS

Except for the short-legged, chubby ones
    that hover at shoulder level
ready to soften your fall after fainting
    into a patch of puncture vines
while hitchhiking the dirt clotted valley road
    you ran out of gas on after work,
the fog colored angels rarely smile, they never
    look you up and down
to measure the shine of your clothes
    or make eye contact, as if
they're rebounding from a nervous breakdown.
    The most I've ever seen at once
were crowded into a hospital service elevator
    rolling dice into the corners
to decide who would be in charge of saving who
    when the code reds were paged.
Once a group of angels was whipping the wing
    of another for stealing fruit cocktail
off the cart of a dead man's tray and another
    was banished to boredom
for napping in the soiled laundry closet and wanting
    to be alone for a few minutes.
My friend, Leonard, saw hundreds of them
    sleeping in lofts of torched farms
while stationed in Vietnam. They were huddled
    together like white turkeys,
coughed and wheezed in unison and when one of them
    woke up and winked at him
he knew he would make it. They are everywhere

and nowhere. I've seen bums
spit at them and watched the hungry elbow them
    out of line at Poverello House:
angels of memory and mist, of mud and lightning,
    angels of orchids and toe jambs,
angels of temper tantrums and lost hair, of tractors
    rust-plastered in a stream of weeds
and of bus stations where people run through them
    and never say, " I'm sorry,
but I've got to get to Long Beach and quick."
    They are all sad
because they have been expelled from heaven
    for annoying God
and think that the world is what it is
    because of they're not working hard enough,
where souls are darkening and spiraling into all that is empty,
    into their recurring fear of doing this forever.

YOU WALK WITH THE SPIRITS

Your car is dead and your toe
has bubbled and blistered up
from too many kicks to the bumper.

The swing shift is over, blood
has twined a crusty nest into this
morning's free-to-run-wild hair

and the drunk whose elbow you braced
to an emergency room chair
must have been the one who vomited

on your shoe. The insects are haggling
with the air and the parking lot
is now empty of squealing tires,

its drivers whizzing through the yellows
and blinking railroad crossings,
traversing three zip codes and five 7-11's

and one-third of a Grateful Dead song
before they can raise their sore feet up
above the level of their hearts to fend off

the traveling migraine before the ice
dilutes their Stoli on the rocks. You
pop the latch, click your Zippo into flame

to scan the cave of hieroglyphics
under the hood, all of which translates
into *hurry, catch the last bus.*

On the corner of Divisadero and San Pablo
under a pavilion of sagging stars,
the moon gliding behind Frontier Chevrolet

and the bottle capped streets so thick
with heat the wind must have lost its whistle,
and through the eerie dark you can hear

the traffic light snapping off and on
to the cadence of a switchblade as if
the devil, were once again, mocking light.

You imagine jazz, the hum of a sax,
a dusty tremolo rounding the night,
a rumor of drums brushing the moon,

the death-raising tingle of vibes. And
whether it's spilling out the back porch
of the mortuary down the alley

when the janitor finishes sweeping up
or if it's just riddling inside your head, it won't
matter. It was invented for bus stops

at midnight. Rahsaad taps your shoulder.
He has been dead since 1977. He sniffs
the air and touches your hospital badge,

thanks you for doing such a good job
of shoveling human shit for a living
and points for you to follow him home.

You're too young to have your things
in order you tell him and he talks of
how at one time he could hear

a cat purring on a stove in the projects,
a mile and a-half from The Santa Fe
Depot and could measure the tides

by its echoed splash against the rocks
and the distance and direction a beer can
was thrown by the sound of its clunk

against the wall. He quickens his funeral march
step as you hold on to his sleeve,
fearful the sun will rise to flesh him out

before he finds the sound he came back for—
wisps of music the wind made in moving
the chimes that hung over his head the minute

he went blind. He heard the squish of shoes
leaving the room and a squall of tears,
lightning sparking the dark spaces between the stars.

THE GERMAN SHEPHERD BLUES

If it's necessary to believe in something then believe
   in the Kingdom of maggots
that the merciless cats have already dug up and pissed on
   or the quirky gecko

poking its prehistoric head out of the ivy patched garden wall.
   I was not meant
to stay in one place, this backyard, to count the pulse
   of the hummingbird

or to spend all night trying to pull cactus thorns
   from out of my paw. I' m tired
of those who say that I'm worth my weight in dry food
   and dirt as a guard dog

when in truth I hate everybody and am always hungry.
   And when the wind blows
from the west I get worse. I bark at shadows buried
   in the wood chips

and can hear rats grinding their teeth just beyond the fence
   and I'll tip over
my tin bucket of a water dish just for the noise and when
   my owner comes out

I'll crack snail shells between my teeth to disgust him.
   When he tries to teach
me to fetch, I keep bringing him my own sun dried turds as a hint
   that I was not given

to playing dead and begging, not like my house-broken sister
    who takes walks
on a leash, sneaks a nap on the recliner, and rolls over for Fritos
    from the kids

who are not allowed to pet me. Some days, when the wind
    currents drift at
just the perfect speed, the hair on my neck bristles and my tail moves
    up like an antennae

and I can pick up the scent of bitch and bone co-mingling
    in the breezes
from a mile away and I start panting like a cornered possum.
    Once I chewed

through a gas line digging myself out only to hear the whiz
    of pellets blocking
my route to that Ava Gardner of a poodle's door. I've listened to stories
    and seen pictures

of gorillas, elephants, big cats and tiny birds, even pandas
    and raccoons
as they peacefully walk the plank toward the Ark and not one
    of my kind in sight.

If a German Shepherd would've had a voice in the Bible,
    we'd all have souls
and a chance at heaven where I, too, could ground my fears
    of the devil and dying,

where I could look out from this prison of a life through cataracts
    and a bad hip

and still want more of this yard carpeted with craters and a matrix
   of rose trellises,

bushels of bougainvillea lapping the windows and me snapping
   at the honeybees
before I circle my bed of privet leaves above the loam of earth
   that will one day soon

nourish my flesh before I go on to refuse to guard the gate
   and herd the angels.

CLEANING UP THE CATHEDRAL

My name is Roosevelt Taylor
and my day begins at midnight
lying on my back across the pews,
shielded by the shadows
of the statues of saints as the moon
splinters the light off the stained
glass into gold arrows of flame.
I wedge a flashlight
between my chin and throat
and brace a double pump
action pellet gun to my shoulder.
I'm a Baptist and shoot pigeons
who roost in the rafters.
I blind them with light
and then aim for their breast.
I hate it when they drop
at the feet of Mary by the altar
or plop into the baptismal fount
as if drowning in a vat of acid.
Sometimes I imagine I'm
on a boat gigging frogs,
paddling through a teeth of reeds,
a buzz of mosquitoes swarming
and patrolling the stars.
Monsignor hired me because
he couldn't find a Catholic to do this
and when I told him that
to pluck and fry a pigeon
was easier than dressing a coot,

I was his man just like the atheist,
Vern, maintenance man by day
and catfish creeper at night.
We make a good pair—
I gunny sack the dead pigeons,
he sweeps up the grey feathers,
and wipes blood stains off the frescoes
before we empty the mouse traps
into the incinerator drum
in the back alley. Once we
had a few too many snorts
and lit our joints off the votives;
and forgot the trap-emptying and they kept
snapping and squealing during mass
after Monsignor had baited them
with his saved and half-crushed wafers.
Maybe it's because he knows
I'm stealing his Camels
from the bottom desk drawer at the
refectory that he doesn't praise me
in the bulletin just before the benediction
or maybe he takes it for granted
that bird droppings won't fall
on the heads of the faithful
during his sermon, or maybe he remembers
me as the one who walked
an old lady down the stairs to the bus stop
after an early morning mass.
She smelled of tangerine blossoms
and we passed right by the alms box.
Birds were chirping, the sky
was blurring when I sat her down

on the bench and left, her hands folded
across a lap of embroidered lilies
and butternut leaves when an over-freighted
semi shifted its weight and crushed
her to the pavement breaking her back,
her legs dangled off the curb
as if from a cushion of clouds
she couldn't rise out of. Morning
shades were popping open, dust
streamed the windowsills. Goose-
necking kids on their bikes
were shooed off to school as Monsignor
said a prayer I've heard many times over
and now, maybe, he sees me as an ending
he wants to forget, that reckless truck
rounding a corner at full tilt,
displacing its load and freeing the spirit
of an old woman viewing the world
from a bus stop, smiling and clutching her purse.

CHESS

Under the wind nudged
    almond blossoms
I spread out a red and black
    checkered cloth
and place it on the bumpy
     surface of the sawed-
     off tree trunk.

In my bag of mixed pieces
     I can hear
the unruly knights chomping air,
    nostrils flaring,
veins twitching to find an empty field
    to leap into

and the ascetic, angular bishops,
    shifting their eyes
    across a plain
of blood-stained fist pumping pawns
    who shout slogans of hate
    toward their opposing likeness
while the isolated king admonishes
    the squat-backed rooks
for not policing its borders and leaving
    the wander-lusted queen
    in jeopardy.

From my folding chair I am playing God
    by moving pieces

from both sides
and because of that, there are no winners
        or losers
only lost and chipped pieces
        and a game
that lasts long into the dark,
        into another spring.

I move when and how the mood
        strikes me:
Which king to blindfold, which to gag,
        whether to rescue
the horse that strayed and got cornered
        on a square
        soon to be set on fire,
or leave its torched carcass as a lesson
        against grazing.

Most of the pawns have now fallen
        shoulder to shoulder
and been dropped into a common coffin,
        black and white
shuffled together, half a nation short
        of a flag planting.

Between moves the blossoms
        turn to fruit,
the untasted fruit rots on the tree,
        falls to the ground
and is boot-heeled by another generation
        of players
in a game that never ends and is not meant
        to be played by angels.

STEALING POMEGRANATES

Fourteen, pimpled, spindly,
and hiding from the cops
who were tipped off
by the birds hovering
and floating over my head
each time I cracked open a skull
of pomegranate as if they, too,
could find inside that burnished
globe of the universe
the bleeding eye of faith,
or a jumble of blood-lacquered pearls
accidentally dug up by kids
in the vacant lot across
from the trailer park—
as if they could witness the color
of earth on fire, shooting
its random sparks into the night,
into the puffy face of the moon,
into the luminous blood
of angels igniting the sky,
causing the sea to swallow
its waves.

When they found me
in the shadow
of the railroad cars stalled
on Tulare Street, waiting
for a sign to move or
change direction, I was

lying on my back
among the oleanders,
one hand fisting a paring
knife, the other covering
my eyes to stop the
fluttering and ticking
as if I'd been dead
before the invention
of shade, tee shirt
smeared red. I could hear
the innards of the box
factory rumble like an
ulcerated stomach when
they asked me why I
stole these when the
Armenian lady
across the alley gives them up
for free. When stolen
I can taste a galaxy
of red stars, the sweetness
of life fermenting in its wounds
into a last rush of sunlight.
I could burn my tongue
on the lava that flowed
through this valley
to form a cocoon of tiny
glowing lamps and watch red
poppies bloom from out
of the Pantheon, my tongue dance
its blazing dance around
the forbidden nipple of Athena.
I could lean my elbow

on a wine smeared table.
I could taste a gateway
to the world, a gateway to sin.

THE BILL COLLECTOR AT SUNRISE

I carry a dust pan
and broom
to sweep the shards
of glass
from the only parking spot
vacant and within view
of the baffled
security guard.
Even though it's too early for the sun
to ladle out light
over the splintered shingles
and empty pizza boxes
tossed to the roof,
I sneak past the one-eared Doberman
chained to the cinder-block
pyramid under the house,
nuzzling its paw.
And too early for the trees
to complain
of their thirst
or drop their sticky petals
on my windshield,
filmed with elm dust.
When I knock,
a young boy in his underwear
tells me the Supermarket
around the corner
has closed for good
and his Daddy took the bus

to the nearest Johnny-Quik
for beer and sodas
and never came back,
leaving his shirts
to soil on the floor.
The cooler keeps rattling
and the shelf-levered TV
has been blaring all night
echoing its voice
across the belly of the pregnant woman
snoring on the couch,
her arm dangling within reach
of the fly swatter.
They know me
by my dog bitten clipboard
and cherry spotted tie
and that I'll be back
before the paperboy
throws the want ads to the front porch,
before those sleep-worthy hands
get untucked
from underneath their cheeks,
and I'll come back guiltless
until I catch a payment
in the surprising spirit of wakefulness.
When I hear
the back door creak
and hear the romping of cats
as they separate the blinds
and scratch at the sill,
I know its time to move on—
donut glaze crusting

my sleeve,
my blank receipt book
sleeping in the trunk,
carrying with it
the promise of tomorrow,
a sureness I share with the sun.

BLACKBERRIES

are god's way of alerting us to the sweet taste of darkness.

From the high branches of oak, 2 crows patiently wait for a disaster
to blossom so they can fan out their smug and savvy wings.

Shacks at the edges of woods were built for their hunting, black
drupelets of coal, raindrops of hot tar concealed by a bramble of

tangled shrubs and tiny arrows of rage caressing its vines, a groved
temple and a house safe for snakes, black widows, and thorns.

The pensive-eyed and elusive lizard searches for a flat spot to hop
while the mockingbird delights in the blood I suck from my fist.

I like them best unripened, hard and bitter, still crusted in their leafy shell,
kernels of ruby sourness sparkling in dew light and river mist, cold

and wild as the rivulets of water flowing beneath their banked roots.

I taste them before the caterpillar and the vinegar fly build their nests
inside their sweetness, before the sores on the lips of the devil turn black.

I watch a young boy and girl fishing under an umbrella of pepper trees.

Their fishing poles are staked in the sand, a pail of worms squirm
in the shade, and a coffee can of unripe blackberries lays within arm's reach.

He clears his caterwauling voice and she shows him her breasts.

A line of blue winged ants, rabid as a father's slap, alight her shoulder.
A blotter of fingerprints streak their faces red, the blushed color of hearts.

THE OWL EXPRESS

Our fingers are padded with soot
and our hats don't fit.
We breathe the same air
the flies have already choked on
and if you are brave enough
to sit with us at the back of the bus
our glares could crumble you
through the challenge of a fight
or the look of one whose face
has been chipped out of ice
or had one too many shock treatments.

We've all been given passes,
carry crazyweed in one pocket,
swiped sugar packets in the other
which we divvy up as if
it were as valuable as a silver compass
or a spray of stars hiding
in the brick shadows of Fulton Street.
Beads of sweat dribble down our necks
and into our shabby collars,
the spine-shivering soon to follow.
At night we want to be left alone,
to bump and glide
around town in circles
because, after all, we're afraid
of the unending horizons, of the dark
and of becoming bats—
a life we all came close to wanting.

Zeke wants to be a penguin
and live in an igloo by the sea,
his puffed out chest
sliding across the ice and never
copping a chill. Ernie
strums his imaginary guitar
and it's all understood
that no one mutters a word about death
when we're almost there
and still no one to invite us in.

The measure and secret of music
are how many devils
it can chase away with its passed down notes
says the fiddle-playing angel,
our mysterious brother
scraping the stars for a song,
gallivanting from one bus stop
to another, always ahead of us
raiding the unlit doorways
and bare bones of banks,
the peeled shutters of all-night cafes.
"Fire and Grace" to the woman
saying good-bye to her sick cat,
a bouncy jig for the limping
streetwalker, a raspy reel
for the dog leashed to a parking meter,
a spicy slide for Carmen
who's sure to come back as a seal,
cracking crab and bouncing
on the ocean's shoulders all day.
And let's not forget

those crisp swings for those
reading from their rented fairy tales
in the haunted corners
of underground parking lots,
those in the windless stop at Courthouse Park,
among the den of bus shelters
and the blossoming nests of tents.
When the sun begins its long walk
up the stairs of the sky
and heaven starts to shed
its skin of darkness, the attendants
wait to take the angel away.
They let him fiddle his way
to the unknown in handcuffs
that glint like glowworms banded
around his wrist. He fiddles a song
no one knows, whistling for more light
and it always comes.

THE MAD WOMAN'S HARP

Before she left she set it there
on the east bank of the Kings,
just below the Rio Vista Treatment Center
and leaned it against the thick, white oak
and slotted its pedals in mud for stability
for all the others like her to easily find
beside the fog-cooled boulder
overlooking the occasional German Brown
jumping for grasshoppers and flies,
to wait for heaven to plant seeds
in their mad fingers so they would match
their own music to the glide of the hawk
veering through the silver framed day
and the wild swan's coast to the notes
of driftwood and nude pianos
in the airy grace of leaves sweeping
through space and never touching earth
inducing the sun to cover its face
behind the Calaveras pine
just long enough for it to catch its breath.

DOG WITH DEMENTIA

There's something about him
    hearing a long train whistle
        under a full moon and the whiff of lilacs
that pulls at the heartstrings
    of old guys like me on their couches
        stooping over to find the remote.
Even the leash
    can't stir him anymore
        and his tail has left its wag far behind.
From eyes that slur the room
    and ears that hover
        to a time long gone
he snorts himself
    out of a dream
        and spots a squirrel
hiding behind the twin lamps
    facing the mantle,
        and his paws are skimming
along the rim of rabbit holes,
    after an all night rain,
        barely padding the ground.
At the hospital
    I had no trouble
        saying good-bye to cancer patients
while spooning out
    their last meal into metallic cheeks,
        pillowing their bruised arms
and drawing light
    out of those hollowed out eyes

                    by telling a risqué story or bad joke.
Now, I adjust his mattress
          to the corner where sunlight will steepen in
                    through the window first thing in the morning;
a pill to sleep
          and a pill to shit
                    and a night-light to trick the dark
before the hibiscus shadow
          frames the wall
                    and walks the room,
before he goes through
          the rigmarole of yawning a breath
                    as if practicing a bark for the last time.

HOUSE WITH AN UNMOWED LAWN

It starts with a beam of moonlight
whitening the knee high grasses
that sprout heavenward,
taller than an untidy tombstone

and as gnarled and spiked
as the sleep-spoiled haircut of one
who is a time zone away
from joining the battle between

coffee and light. The paperboy
keeps shoving the news into the mail
slot because it's his job to probe
through the screen for spiders and dead

flies. The earthworms
are settling into their tunnels
after inking their slime on the sidewalk
and the cockroaches are outrunning

the sun up the porch steps,
past the writhing June bugs
on their backs hissing the stars.
Sure enough someone will dump

a box load of kittens
inside the unlatched gate
to the back steps under the torn
awning that vainly holds the sun

in check. Clothes were crammed
in the hamper, dishrags swayed
and dangled off their pegs, the fried
egg graying under its halo of fat

when they gurney-wheeled you off
with a promise to simplify your life
to a room of your own choosing.
The elm tree stiffens in thirst,

its leaves curling and coiling
into the gutter of the burnt out
streetlamp and the severed sprinkler
erupting each morning at 5

are the only signs of life left
except for the shadow
moving the curtains at night
and the bang of drawers closing,

and the sound of a nail scratching
a chalkboard or a blind man
trying to fit the rusty needle
into the exact groove of his favorite

song. The juniper on the street
that needed you will be cut down.
The roof will be restored
with fresh tar and the cooler

will gloat with new pads and paint.
The cats will grow out of their box

and roam your neighbors' backyards,
leaving mice at your doorstep and your children
to padlock the door, sealing in the emptiness.

ATTICS & THE AFTERLIFE

Loneliness is a wall the dead walk through
when they're looking for company in my attic
of vintage clothes and stacked oak chairs
with hand carved knobs of lion heads
and leather cushioned backs cat-clawed by time.
My uncle wears a hand painted tie of dice
and clasped horseshoes dropping through a red sky.
He shuffles cards to a murmur of clumsy laughter,
a jumble of light enters his veined hands,
bounces off the floorboards and through a crack
in the plaster of my ceiling. He wears a Bulova watch
that hasn't ticked since he was led to the afterlife
and now tells time by measuring shadows.
He is rubbing a shine back into his lost cufflinks
when a flask drops from the secret pocket
of his sport coat and even though it is now always empty
everyone takes a pull, clinks their motel stolen
glasses to the starred hierarchy of angels they aspire to.

They are speaking to each other as clouds must
in the long drawn out syllables of weather, a sighing
vowel for wind, a throat clearing cough for thunder.
They sort through a pile of yellowed newspapers
that the rats have chewed into a nest to lactate their young.
Mrs. Weber refuses to drape her shoulders
in her needle pointed shawl because the rose has faded
and smells like mothballs and menthol. My uncle
lights another imaginary cigarette with his invisible lighter
and blows out smoke as if it were a miracle. They

read their obituaries to find out what the weather was like
the day they died and are disappointed so little was written
about them, how Mrs. Frye drove her grandson to rehab
until he got cured of the shakes, or Miss Thomas re-shingled
her house by herself in the deadening August heat,
or anything about Mr. Granz's death march through the Philippines.
Nothing about Mr. Eagles' heirloom tomatoes.
When I open the door I am met by a circle of dusty coats
and moldy dresses and the necks of hangers
where their faces should be, as if waiting for someone
who just got here to open their eyes.

THE BIRTH OF LIGHT

The last bit of moonlight beams
   through the window
and down the throats of bartenders
   and the swing shift
operators at Zacky Farms, done
   with the last minute butchering
and incubating as they slip into
   the couched sleep of waving

grasses and dying stars, coughing up
   what's left of the dark.
To be walking down Van Ness at this time
   is to scare the stars.
To listen in on the undecided clouds as they
   confer with the night
about the blood lines singeing the eyes
   of farmers and flower vendors

as they curse the shoulder that refuses
   to pivot and twirl
and the back that has lost its torque
   when unloading the trucks,
is to eavesdrop on secrets that will
   one day form dreams,
like a stillness that inhabits the Chinese elms
   before a storm

that might awaken the half-dead kittens tossed
   in empty oil drums

or the security guard lying torpid on the green linoleum
     tiles of the bank,
mulling over the tyranny of alarm clocks
     and the whereabouts of his thermos.
I watch a checkerboard of lights wink on from
     the gray-scabbed apartments,

releasing a littered nebulae of tossed magazines,
     an Early Times bottle,
armfuls of plastic hampers and flattened cardboard
     into the scrapped shopping cart
while a woman stands at the bus stop, allowing
     a pre-dawn breeze
to comb her hair, practicing smiles and mouthing
     the gawky syllables of bliss.

And I go on loving these loveless hours
     like no other before the sun
takes its rightful place at the head of nature's table,
     bronzing the sky,
conning the day, and sending a new shift of angels
     to change the time
on the marquee scanning the ballpark, the hand of heaven
     changing gloves.

III

TOPIARY

Between the blue sage and bottlebrush the alligator points its languid eye upward, toward the sun-cracked clothespins as if it were waiting for Mae West to descend the stairs shifting her trochaic hips and showcasing that meat-fresh curl of the lip and nasty sneer. It remains as still as a knotted and fallen plank. A fly crawls into the leafy pouch of its snout, and as I carve and trim I hear an erratic rustle coming out of the depths of the overgrown privets and see the gator's tail violently whipping the air while the rest of its body waits.

I am scissoring the teardrop leaves from the mule's hoof I rode at West View Park in Pittsburgh. My uncle, saint of my childhood, is chain smoking Luckies and blowing smoke rings into the petals of savanna flower and fake tumbleweed, waving off the bedeviled blackbirds as they dive into the balky wheat of my hair before the sleep-walking mule stepped on his foot, puffing it up to the size of a small watermelon. He continued to lead the mule and me across two square miles of make shift grasslands, past a maze of monkeys squealing for their pailful of fruit, the open mouthed hyenas, the puzzled cheetah, the lazy llama, and curious antelope. After three bus changes, a cream soda at the 5 & Dime, and an envious peek at the colored TV's in the store front windows, he carried me on his shoulder, limping down hill toward home, grinning at each kick to his ribs. I could almost hear him braying.

From the fifth step of the ladder I am trimming the cypress furred neck of the giraffe who is peering over the fence at a landscape of strewed lawn mower parts, leaky batteries, and flattened beer cans. This time I am shaping memories out of the shrubs and bushes of leaves that refuse to die, each new growth an exaggeration of what was always there, for Alexis and her two younger siblings from the projects on their first trip to

Chaffee Zoo. They are gathering eucalyptus leaves for the big-hearted giraffe to lick out of their tiny hands with his black tongue as they scream in terror and joy. I don't know if twenty years from now they'll remember the white guy from Mental Health Services who led them to the train whistle and duck pond at Lake Washington, through the twinkling lights and carnival music of the merry-go-round as they held on to each other for dear life, not knowing that they were, at least for a little while, tricking time.

If owls dream, I don't want them dreaming of me. Like mice and bad weather I am afraid of them. Even the gnats veer off course to avoid their eyes and whirl around the ears of something safer. If one perches on your roof, someone close to you will die. If one lands on your porch and peers into your bedroom window, someone inside will die in their favorite chair before the next full moon. And, heaven help you, if one gets trapped inside your house and nests in your attic, the owl will sever your windpipe with its claws while you sleep. I cannot trust someone who watched Christ being crucified and then sat on the cross while he and the other two boiled away in the sun, and did nothing. And yet, in many ways, I want to be like them: shadowy and completely carnivorous, carrying secrets of the night beneath the wings of a noiseless flight, appearing out of nothingness, a voice tiptoeing through the darkness from limb to limb between the blue needles of the hemlock, high above it all and almost invisible.

Between gaps in the four-poster Chinese wisteria vine Chris, Soto, Gary, and I are trailing the free wheeling stars, measuring the spaces of light between one darkness and another as clouds stretch out of nowhere to roof the sky. Out of the blue star juniper bush I have sculpted two oxen, a garland of red and green chilies yoking their necks, to shoulder a rose root twined table. On the table, coals are glowing from the hibachi as we plaster the chicken legs with a secret marinade. A boatload of beer is cooling in the puddle of almost melted ice and we are using cow skulls as bongo drums and beating on them with garden tools, ignoring the hiss of June bugs and spittle of snails. We are pretending to be immortal. When we sing, we stir the bones of birds I've buried in the back garden. It is loud enough for the dead to laugh at our frenzied plans.

WIND

My love for wind began in the fourth grade when it entered our school
as nature's kind uncle with a bad temper. It popped out all the windows,
then blew the roof off, billowed up the skirt of Mrs. Means who was
leading us to shelter and in prayer, the buckles of her girdle exposed to
those of us brave enough to open our eyes. My favorite part was no school
for two weeks and now I think of how it unites me to my dead friends.
I can't remember the dates of their deaths but I can remember at what
level and velocity it was blowing at their funerals. For instance it was a
hot and still day for Omar's service except for a parachute gust moving
the treetops, as if his spirit was now sitting in its theatre of oaks with a
cigarette and a beer and that crooked smile that will always be attached
to a passing cloud. And even though it's had its unforgiving side: the kite
tucked in the high power lines, a child born crazy under its violent squall,
the strayed hot air balloon, the hiker losing its balance at a great height,
a ship toppling over in the Baltic; I've yet to read an obituary where
someone was killed by wind or leaves their money to a wind relief fund.

Forget about taking on the spirit of the seagull with its freedom-loving
wingspan, its incessant squawk, and its mob mentality in skimming the
sand for dropped saltines; or the telescopic-eyed owl gliding and gleaning
the riverbank for snakes and rats. Forget about that silly old man chasing
a whale, or Picasso, or becoming the first fair, foreign-born President of
any country. I want to come back as wind, the product of angels pumping
their legs around the clock, squirrel-like, in heaven's cage. I would be the
foamed squall that rinses the rocks and the awkward breath of a breeze
cooling the backs of first time lovers in the bed of a pickup outside a
cantaloupe field in Firebaugh. I'm already thinking of stealing money
from the hands of beachgoers as they order margaritas from the Cantina
de la Reina and blowing and scattering those five-dollar bills down the

boardwalk just for a few laughs. No one would know where I was going or where I came from, even though they pretend to, from the nightly newscaster to the spit glazed finger held up to the sky gods to test my power.

I've put away thoughts about being the next Einstein, or Napoleon, or Babe Ruth in the next life. I'm heir to the wind. Dark as a tunnel and as lucent as a star on fire in a wintry sky. Ageless and heavier than I look, I'll continue to extinguish the flames of young and old alike. Even the sun cannot talk me down; or the moon handcuff me. I'll be gravity's repulsive and non-compliant self, fire's nightmare, and drought's hope, God's maniacal and mysterious favorite.

THE BIRTH OF MUSIC

Fires were always burning, day and night, in the large circle in the center of the village. Everyone had a job: fire stokers, animal skinners, thatch builders, plant tenders, tunnel routers where on one side of the river they stored food, and stacked the dead on the dead—herbalists, irrigators, and at the top, hunters. Soldiers hadn't been invented yet as we knew of no enemies. We were divided into groups, each group had an assigned time to pray and prayed to many different gods dependent on what was bothersome to them at the time: god of maize, of bruised fingernails, of colliding clouds, of tree hanging snakes, or afternoon shadows; god of coddled children, of beauty, of rapture, and scorn. This, too, went on day and night. As long as the fires kept glowing and they continued praying there would always be a sun and moon. An official time-spelling magician who would close his eyes and put himself into a trance in order to imagine water dripping through his eye sockets into the back of his skull, designed the rotating of prayer shifts, and he would measure time by the level of water slogging in his brain. We, as children, would gather sticks for the fire and save a good one for ourselves, usually from the hornbeam tree, and burn its tip so after a dinner of burnt boar flank, a bucket of charred tree creepers, and a blood pudding made by slicing the fresh throats of sparrow hawks with a dash of peppered wasp; we would, with our charcoal tipped sticks draw, what we saw of the world on rocks and boulders. Once, on a weather-limed cliff, I saw the drawing of a gigantic bear standing on its hind legs, its head higher than the pines, devouring a man the size of a fish.

I was warned not to wander beyond the first line of trees where the horizon and earth became one and where caged between the beeches and berries the world dropped off into a crater of fallen rocks, roots, and bloated tigers whose eyes had been gouged out by the fires of devils carrying torches. I couldn't tell if it was the trees doing the humming or the wind having found the soft pocket of their leaves to home into, but I got lost with the moon at my back and the stars ushering me into a forbidden darkness I was trying to whistle my way out of. I heard gags and sobs of another lost from their village and then another and another, all of us talking in different clicks and clacks, notes of our longing, a clattering of fears we whittled into bark whistles, rabbit boned flutes, and a kudzu looped harp, and instead of fisting our foreheads we drummed out sticks and hollowed out logs to create a language of rhythms that we moaned between blazes of feet and space we later called dance. Every so often we met up with another who had also wandered too far and whose fear was lessened by mimicking the tempo of the wind. Crows that nested in the tree forks, ready to plunge into the red flecked sky and the stunted clouds, became familiar with us now as we went from village to village trading our songs for tanned hides, mead, and a roll in the hay, which made us forget we were lost. We walked and when we sang the bulging maze of the world became smaller, the moons countable. Flakes of light dusted our shoulders, ghost moths fluttered before our faces, beeswax and honeysuckle jumbled our senses; a sprinkling of notes wheeled us on, singing us home.

PIGEON IN A PALM TREE AT ROEDING PARK

I fly up here each day at dusk after the squadron of hawks has veered off down the railroad tracks to scavenge the boxcars full of dead chickens and grain, and just before that black-nerved and soulless owl makes its rounds under the bobbing stars, before the sky turns dark as a coma. I come here to watch the thin fabric of earth turn a different shade of green, to hear the snoring breath of God while he naps, and to erase the thoughts of death I've built up throughout the day—the kid slinging darts, the cat that lunges from out of the bushes, the escaped goose pecking at my eye while I forage the ground for sesame twigs and thistle seeds. Earlier a Frisbee whooshed my throat feathers right in the middle of my cooing. It is as solemn as lent when the low-riders wax their cars under the biscuit of a full moon. Their tattooed arms muscling out the blemishes of their pride until the moon reflects their faces in the shine of the winged fury streaming atop their hood ornaments. The fountain in the corner track reminds me of rain and the possibility that I might live forever, how it buries the leaves into the earth later to return as trees, how the water bubbles break up the sludge, giving light to tadpoles and perch, and guppies while uncovering the bodies of sacked pets. The low-riders roll their cuffs up to feel for coins in their bare feet. They divide their loot up and throw the pennies back into the raining fountain. I can read their wishes in the bleeding creases of their eyes.

3 TREES

Ernesto wasn't embarrassed to admit that he loathed physical labor, exercise of any kind. This came from a man who was beautiful, trim, whose childhood dream was to be a flamenco dancer, whose father trained boxers in Mexicali. Once he volunteered to haul boulders up an embankment for our friend to build a retaining wall in Santa Cruz. He kept stopping midway up the hill to discuss the varied translations of Neruda, wondering how he might treat this as a poetry inspiring experience: an ode to the grandeur of rocks or one that invoked the pathos of the oppressed worker.

When Ernesto bought a house with a gone-to-swamp swimming pool, roses in their death beds, uncared for fruit trees on an one acre back yard plot I was only too glad to help him move, a one day project that took two weeks because of his effervescent stalling tactics: I'm thirsty, I'll buy you a beer at the Silver Dollar; this beer made me crave salt, let's stop at the 7-11 for sunflower seeds; I'll need to order Chinese take out for lunch and maybe a nap break afterwards. I had deep concern for his yard and I shouldn't have. I should have known that Ernesto would never let anything waste away and die if he could help it. The pool ended up meeting his Hollywood standards, the roses showed off their bounty of colors, the withered fruit trees lapped up water once again and new ones were planted. I never asked him how he did this because I knew he didn't know.

There's a black and white photo that his wife Diane took of him acting the part of a land baron farmer. He's wearing Levis and a denim shirt rolled to the elbows, his arm attached to a shovel. The trouble is that he's wearing dress loafers, designer sunglasses and the shovel is upside down. Once after a long day of teaching he came over to my house, concern etching his face. He told me he had a confession to make that plagued all weak-charactered men, right away I knew he shouldn't have taken that teaching gig and made himself vulnerable to those students whom I knew would adore him. I sat down, ready to hear about his involvement with a young heroin addict, ready for him to show me his sleeve-covered tracks. But all he said was that he felt guilty of buying a quart of ice cream from Thrifty's for his family that night and had finished eating the whole thing by the time he got to my house a mile away. I suggested he buy another quart from a classier parlor and offered my services as a sponsor and interventionist.

I've planted a tree in my backyard in his memory. It's a tree only he and I can see and he's welcome to it anytime. It's an ice cream tree and with it I've left a can of butterscotch syrup and a spoon. I don't bother to unlock the gate because I know he's now light enough to pass through anything. When I hear the spoon clanging, the humming and crowding of bees in the arbor, I'll go outside to taste that sweetness once again and we'll go on from where we left off—the sky inking tranquility and the orange flame of the moon raging with envy at our butterscotch smiles, laughing as if there was no such thing as death.

• • •

Moulton was a grizzly bear with bad teeth who rode a motorcycle. He looked as if children had scribbled games of tic-tac-toe on his face as he snored on the couch, and when he smiled he could spotlight a dark forest. His face should've been carved into Rushmore apart from the other four and looking into a different direction, accepting all the chaff the wind could throw his way. No matter what his age, he always looked older.

My dog loved him, perked up his ears each time he heard a motorcycle, kids loved him, bankers and bartenders, the homeless, and the guy owning a view of the bluffs; I'm sure bats and wolves as well. Moulton was very proud of his arrest record. Once, upon release, he walked past a Hmong refugee who looked lost and disoriented at a bus stop. He put his arm across his shoulders and pointed to the bevy of men in suits lugging briefcases, lectured the refugee through his gravelly voice, "see those guys over there, they're twice as scared as you and their future looks like shit." Despite the language barrier the man looked like he understood Moulton—which was rare even in English—then accepted a ride on his motorcycle.

Moulton would set up shop at the College Union selling in-depth astrological horoscopes for five dollars as he advertised on a square of cardboard scribed with crayons. If you didn't have five dollars he would do a quick analysis for a cup of coffee and if you didn't want your fortune told he would do it for free, which is what he did for me and after a six month analysis, he called and said I could do whatever I wanted and when I asked if that was all he could come up with after all this time he said, "yep, buddy boy, it's like a rap sheet from the planets and it's all they have on you."

For as long as I can remember Moulton always had trouble with his teeth which were false and that he carried in a pliant black case clipped to his belt as if they were handcuffs. Once when he was hosting a poetry radio show, which he had asked me on as a guest, he just took them out and read a poem of mine, gumming the lines. Then he left me in charge while he tried to borrow another set from the technician's father, as I found out later. Another time they flew out while he was reciting a soliloquy as a lead character in a Shakespeare play.

When he died we planted two pistache trees on the corner of Olive and Linden in the Tower District and buried with it a couple handfuls of coffee beans donated by Java Cafe, his favorite hangout. I regret not walking through the Tower District where Moulton was an iconic figure and not asking for other mementos to bury: extra spark plugs for his next ride, keys to a garage which stored an old sofa he could crash on, a shot glass, a book of James Wright's poems from the used bookstore, a hippie-fringed vest from the thrift store, a rusted church key from the antiques' peddler. I've planted a tree in my yard that grows teeth so that when he comes over with his knapsack of poems and apples, and picks a ripe set off the tree, whittles away the peel and eats the apple, core and all. He'll bring out his poems and read in the voice I first heard at Cafe Midi when he read to post bail money for a friend. The wind will change direction; the tooth tree will clack like silver chimes against the background of stars tumbling backwards into a distinct sky bruised with drama.

. . .

Omar was a brother in poetry and organ meats. Sometimes I think we spent as much time discussing the flavor able merits of a delicately spiced and baked pig's snout as on the poetry of Byron. I loved sitting in Omar's backyard eating a breakfast of eggs, potatoes, beans, and buche; halving an avocado from his tree, sprinkling it with a fresh lemon from one of his lemon trees, then using the avocado shell as an ash tray afterwards.

If there were a wind it would sigh. The birds would turn their beaks up at us, especially when they thought we had tricked them into believing our platefuls of fried tripe were not a lottery of worms. It was as if the darkness of the world had quickly moved to a place outside of our selves. During his life Omar survived many catastrophes. When I once asked him what he attributed this life-enhanced quality to, he said he was born with a resilient gene and menudo.

Without me telling him Omar always seemed to know when I didn't have a job. He would come over with a huge jar of his second mother's homemade menudo and this was usually complemented by another dish—a frozen chicken, a can of olives, a few over ripe bananas. We would eat till we sweat the poverty out of our pores. It was definitely a dish loaded with mood enhancers as we began to talk so fast we couldn't understand each other but knew whatever we were postulating was brilliant.

His family called me one day to tell me Omar was in ICU care at a local hospital. When I got there the priest was already giving what I assumed to be Last Rites. I came again the next day to find his bed empty and when I inquired about his passing the nurses said that he's not dead, he's fine and in another room entertaining and flirting with the nurses. I was so excited to see him I gave in to his wish to bring him something to eat from the outside so long as it didn't oppose doctor's orders. I brought him a lengua burrito and when I cut it in half it smelled—I'm sure and Omar agreed—of God boiling potatoes in heaven.

In the last six months of his life I took him to a Mexican restaurant that served all-you-can-eat menudo on Tuesdays. We made a mess of the place—oregano spilled into our bowls like rain from a leaky roof, onions squished between our teeth, and the chili flakes so hot our ears caught fire. We ate like it was our last meal, and it was. It was the last time I ate with Omar.

It was Omar's publishers-clearing-house dream to own a ranch. The house would be encircled by a wide, flower-potted porch, so he could have a different view of his sad-eyed cows each day. There would be plenty of hired help to freshen his ice tea during the long afternoons. When I come to visit him there I'm going to bring a tripas tree to plant—cabeza, sesos, trotters, and honeycomb tripe, all the unwanted parts will blossom and flicker like magic. The stars will light up one by one and we'll be as serene as the droopy-eyed moon smacking its lips.

• • •

Everyone needs a tree to talk to and I've got three. It'll be a community of wind that brings us back together on a Friday morning to the Chicken Pie Shop. Moulton will choose from his bushel a set of teeth to accommodate a square of cherry cobbler and a side of cinnamon, which he'll snort to clear his sinuses. Omar will work on his liver scrambler and I'll have a go with the gizzard stew. A mound of chocolate pudding graced with an acre of whipped cream will leave a mustachioed film on Ernesto's upper lip. We'll, once again, begin reinventing our lives over platefuls of imaginary truths, buttering our bread with soul.

ANGELS AT BUS STOPS

When rain is the scratch of fingernails
across the moon's face,

and the wind sears the treetops
stapling its eyes shut,

the angels have a tough time
telling time

or in what direction they're
supposed to be transporting the dead.

I've watched them limp
into boxcars brimming with sacks

of dirt crusted potatoes,
ready to lift a supine, hung over,

and mistaken saint
into the smoke-stacked air

of south Fresno, and once
you thought Marty the wino

was buried alive under a cardboard coffin.
 Rain tilts my umbrella toward a lost afternoon

of darkened windows in coffee shops
and flooded canals,

its weed-tangled bottom
shimmering with silver hand guns

perceived by the angels
to be the jeweled perch of Jesus.

When they come up behind me
I don't know if I'm dead or alive.

They shrug their wings as if to say,
taking care of the dead is harder than you think.

Even the padlocked taco trucks
and check cashing parlors

on South Van Ness look worn out,
their windows veiled in soot

each starless time
the train whistle pulses through,

their souls sawed into streamers
with the dull blade of money.

In the bone chilling emptiness
of November a woman

in a black hat and overcoat
is fumbling for change

at the leafless bus stop on First Street,
her husband with his rooster crowned hair

mumbles to the unpeopled sidewalk
in his native Estonian

that the chimes of winter
have just begun their steady climb

to a tumultuous crescendo. Bus
stop angel, who walks me

from cover to cover, through
rain and bad dreams,

how often you remind me that
I got here by the message you sent

from that bus stop to Pittsburgh
to my mother to reunite her

to her refugee friends and a job,
I have followed you since then

through the cold and deepening
puddles, toward any tunnel you choose,

breathing in the mist of your wings,
the shoulders of heaven hidden

behind the soggy clouds
and dark grille of the sky.

A SMALL SUITCASE

I could tell they'd never make it
by the way she hugged me
to the breast
that wasn't feeding the boy.
After two years of being tracked
by German soldiers in black uniforms
and Russians in brown
with red trim and black belts,
after being tossed from one
crowded boat to another,
I'm tired of them
drumming on my skin
each time a bomb goes off
a hundred meters away—
tired of crossing the frigid waters
I've lost count of,
and of watching
children cough up blood
onto the freshly fallen snow.
They must be desperate
to have that chatterbox
of a four year old blond girl
lug me through the line
of another refugee camp
only to have their dreams blackened
by another customs agent
who won't be bribed by the silver
spoons I carry in the tattered
pouch of the lining I share
with the death certificate

of God knows who, and the eye-
glasses of a nearsighted professor
who these omen-led Estonians
believe still holds enough
vision to lead them to America.
If they get that far,
they'll need more than luck
to hold them up,
more than waking up
without the blanket they left behind,
with their left feet planted
in the earth upon rising
before the sun
teases them with light.
They'll need more
than the sack of coins
I carry and the herring they'll
eat on New Years and the crows
they'll drive off their sills.
The hysterical one will once again
throw herself into the water
and the others will follow
with me bearing all they own,
like a small, bloated mule,
praying I'll keep them afloat.
The sea will foam,
the gulls will scream,
and they'll wave off all help.
And I'll be thrown
in the nearest ash can
or washed up and left leaning against
the sea-battered feet
of The Statue of Liberty.

FLEEING ESTONIA

The seas grew larger and the houses and stars
   got smaller and smaller.
The moon's cheek will never puff out and shine
   in the same light again.

It's best not to think of what was left behind:
   the buried silver, the rabbit-
furred shawl that warmed your mother's shoulder,
   or the braid snipped

from the one curl of your sister's hair now lost
   to the wind. Forget
the puzzled frown on your dead husband's brow,
   or the stand of alder trees

having lost their green, and the birch bark thumb nailed
   with packets of snow—
their shimmering coats reflecting a forest of resinous
   amber and full moons.

• • •

The wind is a shuttle to the sea, and the sea a home to die in.
The Russians are standing on tops of trains to pick off
stragglers who cough and wheeze and quote the Psalms.
These checkpoints used to be tree-lined corridors,
a border of bees guarding their honey so fiercely
that no farmer would cross it in spring,
no wind would dare violate its stillness at dusk.

They shot Kaido clinging to an oak branch,
his body easing into the snow one limb at a time
while the train whistles its echo of grief,
and the smoke of rifle fire clouds the frozen sky.

• • •

Winter is winter in any language or any place
    they hope to land.
All these tangle of strangers with their roped boxes
    know what cold is.

Snow is topping the crown of The Statue of Liberty
    as we scan the shore,
closing our eyes to snap in her wind scarred face
    to a new memory,

hoping that God will remember us despite our
    scavenging food and money
from the belts of dead soldiers who we cannot forgive
    for not running far enough.

The world will always be a forest of eyes peering out
    from the barbed wire
encampment. It must be the wind-demented waves that
    make us want to remember

their faces; and the sad-eyed milk cow waiting for its daily
    stroll among the stubble
of winter wheat and the yellowed heads of rutabaga
    popping out of the earth.

Forget the night of rats outside your window gnawing
    on horseflesh and bone,
the brick dust that was once your house, the freewheeling
    blackbirds jousting

the hawks for tree space, even the toboggan runs
    down the moonlit roads
of your childhood. It's time to pray to the Morning Star
    and wash your feet in clover.

                                                    • • •

The chewing gum the American soldiers
handed out was swallowed in hunger.
No need now to fake fear or silence
as they checked inoculations, visa papers,
and sponsoring permits. We have nothing
to offer the Italians when they share
their coffee and cigarettes but a hand
on a shoulder when they weep for an ocean
floor peppered with their dead. The snow
is stinging our fingers and your mother
must be scraping ice from the icicled
kitchen window as she awaits your return.
We count the smokestacks stoking
and graying the sky in a city that
must have lost its gloves in the frigid,
rolling waves of winter—
loud and treeless, opening its windows
for us to enter with our newly formed voices.

THE ETHEREAL COFFEEMAKER

From my mattress bed on the floor
I hear my uncle rise from his bed
to make coffee, his bare feet sliding
across the green-checkered linoleum.
The cat is lapping from its white bowl
and the dog is chewing on the doorknob
while my uncle measures out six
spoonfuls into a small, silver basket
that will soon ease into mud,
and smell like the mist-perfumed wing
of the seagull that slices through the fog
outside our window into the manzanita shrub.
When I hear the matchstick scraping
my uncle's fingernail; and the whoosh
of the stove exhaling gas into a tick of flame,
I know the natural waking order of the world
will soon be restored despite what the radio
whispers: A volcano destroys a city
whose name I can't decipher,
a union leader in Kentucky is shot
walking his daughter to school
and his wife will bury him where she thinks
he'll hear the whippoorwill chirp at night.
A stream is drying up in South America
and the Russians are gaining ground
on their way to another planet. I count
one-thousand-one, one-thousand-two;
wait for those loam-like granules to dribble
upward into a brown bubble of a star,

gurgling and shining in the dark;
a toy spaceship undocking from its chamber.
If my count goes beyond seventy-five before
the perking stops, my uncle will live
forever; if seventy-five or less, I will die
before him and for today, after our first sip,
before the sun shows off its perfect shine,
I'm beaming and the toast is popping
because I've willed death to stand alone,
apart and outside of ourselves.

My uncle has been dead a long time now.
My coffeemaker doesn't percolate, but groans.
The water boils down instead of up,
each drop a trickle of time I can't reverse
no matter how hard I imagine. The lone
egg will have to wait for the weekend
to mix it up with the buttered hash browns
and slabs of cardboard-laced bread.
Outside, the twin maples are browning
and the roses are releasing their fire-red
petals to the washed out October sky.
A murmur of bees lies at the feet
of the cactus blossom, a mayhem of ants
circling their lacerated wings.
In my saggy boxers and with an arthritic
shoulder, I throw dirt clods at the woodpecker
who keeps hammering up grubs and sawdust
and who never flinches from me,
who crouches among the shadows of pokeweed
and telephone poles.
I go inside to measure the drops of coffee

that sink into a past of wind wings
and two-tone paint jobs and Chesterfields.
I fry up three pieces of bacon,
a devil's face at the window for each piece,
and dip a biscuit into the grease,
wait for the swash of steam to announce
itself to my palate-puckering, cynical lips.
I forget about hiding the ashes of my remains
in with the coarsely ground Italian Roast,
and later as emulsion for the tomatoes.
Today I'm going to drink my bitter coffee,
munch on bacon, and dredge up the past,
the distance between doing both and doing nothing
is infinite. Today I'm going to live forever.

PUMPERNICKEL

When I eat pumpernickel bread
I am a young boy pumping
my butter-fattened legs
toward the farmhouse,
past the slate stacked sauna,
through the undulating wheat
and peat-smoked bogs,
the mist rattling the leaves off
the alder and white birch
into a mix of water and wind.
I find you culling the blackberry vine,
urging the oats to roll themselves,
the shovel always at your side,
an ally to wrestle the cabbage heads with.
White flour has gummed
the wild hair of your arms
into tiny globes of snow,
bees dance on your neck
and when you kick at the millions of moths
that invade your rye each year
I watch your eyes flame
from the dust of their wings
as you throw your pocket watch at them
into a splash of mud. Grandfather,
I have no need to build
a straw cave anymore
or learn how to start
a fire without matches.
The black geese have long ago floated

into the driftwood they were born into
and where I live there are no storks
living in the church belfry
hovering over their clutch of eggs,
their beaks clattering,
alerting us to the revival of beetroot,
the loitering of spring.
But I can still remember
how to predict the hour of rain by dividing
the sky into twelve squares,
picking out the dark ones, then
adding to it the wing beats of a goldeneye duck.
Each day I come home for lunch
and knife into the hard crust of pumpernickel,
its center as sour and dark as God's pain,
and I cover it with a small boatload of herring
and for twenty minutes,
between noon light and dream light,
I watch you pour
scalded milk over butter, sugar, salt,
muttering to the caraway seeds,
triple kneading the dough,
then throwing the leftover grains
out the window, some of which
will take to the earth,
others to be carried by the wind
across four countries and two wars
and beyond uncountable, borderless waters
to land at my kitchen table,
where you inhabit
the pungent taste of pumpernickel,
a seeded taste I refuse to spit out.

FLIES

Tiny chip of coal
broken off
from the devil's tooth.

Fleck of black agate
escaping out of the cove
of a mummy's nose.

Your song
is universal. Misery
is your drone.

Prison cooks
hide your carcasses
inside their rice pudding.

Fat guys on porches
wave their hats at you
and shotgun blast your summer.

Lost puzzle
piece of soul,
my mother was arrested

for not saluting Hitler
in 1939. She was forced
to write a letter

praising him. She
wanted to warn the others
that she saw a fly

clamped to his
right temple and no matter
how much he waved

and shouted
the fly wouldn't unglue
its clawed feet

from his forehead,
just below the hairline.
She took this

as a sign of evil.
One with compound eyes,
snake fly, sawfly,

stonefly, whitefly, or one
who tastes with their feet,
there's a lot for a kid to like:

never rests, never tires,
one who walks on ceilings
and is quicker than my cat,

more enduring
than any student in annoying
Mr. Emmert when he tried

to make sense of Algebra,
and I can't count the times
I tested my reflexes

against your elusive wings
only to have my palms smeared
with death's goo.

Blood lapper,
pollen piercer,
all in all,

Lenny Bruce had it wrong
when he said
he had a cousin

who gave the clap
to two guys
and nobody whacks her

with a newspaper.
Black pearl locked
in Zeus' lidded jar,

I saw you flying
among a squadron of others,
your swarm broken by slaves

across an East African plain
with eight foot fans
across the sultan's face

and then, again, on every news clip,
that's given me a bad dream—
the soldier watching his leg

float down the Mekong without him,
crows sifting through the soot
of another car wreck,

dogs with crusted eyelids
and chewed off ears,
caged and waiting to be saved—

it's easy not to forget
your indelicate link
in this chain of suffering.

THE ROCKING HORSE

So why was he crying?
God hadn't invented
thunder yet. War was
a whisper among aunts
and no one had told him
that his father was dead
and he was to spend
the rest of his life looking
into the clouds for him.
On cold nights he pressed
his cheek against the paint-
chipped harbor of the horse's
neck, gold sparks speckling
his tiny hands as he bridled
the red flag of his tongue
until the horse's wild
and dark eye led him through
the cross beam that latched
the attic door and between
the mullion-paned window.
Outside, among the drooping
branches of birch,
the wind's echo and the bomb-
leveled forest, alongside
flashes of light tunneling the sea,
angels nodding off
in the treetops and over-ripe
gooseberries splotching their faces,
he and the horse

split the road between death
and beauty until the horse's eye
lost its luster and they trotted
home, the boy asleep,
his face carved into the horse's mane,
to spoonfuls of honey
and jellied pork. Why
did they have to leave him there,
the boy thought when the soldiers
hurried them into the boat
and threw the horse onto the wood pile?
The boy couldn't blot out
the picture he now saw of the horse
lying on its side,
spider webs scaling his ears,
rat paws scrolling his eye,
his forelegs being axed
by a one-armed guard,
kindling for a book burning.

WOMAN AT A RED TABLE

After a painting by Leon de Smet

The houses on the canal bank
get smaller each day and the mist
shimmers through the church of ginkgos

and beeches toward a road
that no one has passed
in a long time, not since

before the war when I rode up
in a horse driven carriage
on my wedding day, red-cheeked

and happy, the dogs yelping
at the horses' hooves. I was
bundled in a fur coat that I later

bribed the Nazis with before
they pointed me to the North Sea.
Every day I think of how far

he must have walked in the snow
before they shot him or whether
he coughed himself to death.

Yet each day I wait,
say grace by habit and try
to remember the stars we named

or where in the attic
we hid the cocoa and honey.
With my good foot

I search for the spoon I dropped
before the ants crawl to it
in single file. Even the flowers

are drowsy and blurred,
peony indistinguishable from poppy,
rose from camellia, as if

my featherbrained neighbor,
on her morning walk, had cut
them off from a sky singing with light,

and vased them next to a folder
discarded by a husband
rushing off to catch a train

or a teen-aged son
running off to school
and forgetting his homework.

I strum my fingers
against the teapot
because it reminds me

of the click and clack dance
of migratory birds
mating atop my chimney

and I only leave
to buy earrings and a new dress
each summer,

when the lane of maples
outside my window
have inhaled all the darkness,

then I re-paint the table red,
try to sand out and bury the long nights
and rekindle the mercies of dawn.

FOREST IN TWILIGHT

for my father

I walk through the fast and fading light
that once flamed red on the forest floor.

There were times I prayed for you to return,
for the clouds to lower you through the mist

of umbrella pines into a grove of birches
where you'll cushion your head against

their moon grilled silver trunks. Your cheeks
dabbled with firethorn and your hands scribbled

with cuts from the gooseberry bush
and a hunger you couldn't have forgotten.

Many times I've asked to trade places with the dead
just to sit next to you on the alder stump

counting catkins and breaking open hazelnuts
with stones we fashioned as arrowheads.

You'll chuckle at all my failures
and I'll point out how differently the light would glide

through dog star and cloud breath
had you stuck around or come sooner

when I called out for you
to fill in the blanks of a dark and twisted sky

and how I've waited for you in this breakneck glide
of sunset, this lifetime of heart cracking light.